Milkshakes 101

Your Guide To Making The Ultimate Milkshake Recipes Ever!

By

Ted Alling

Copyright 2016 Ted Alling

License Notes

No part of this Book can be reproduced in any form or by any means including print, electronic, scanning or photocopying unless prior permission is granted by the author.

All ideas, suggestions and guidelines mentioned here are written for informative purposes. While the author has taken every possible step to ensure accuracy, all readers are advised to follow information at their own risk. The author cannot be held responsible for personal and/or commercial damages in case of misinterpreting and misunderstanding any part of this Book

Table of Contents

Introduction 5
Sweet Milkshake Recipes 7
Sweet Brownie Batter Milkshake 8
Delicious Banana Foster Milkshake 10
Classic Oreo Milkshake 13
Decadent Red Velvet Milkshake 15
Chocolatey Mudslide Milkshake 17
Kit Kat Milkshake 19
Sweet S'mores Milkshake 21
Frozen Hot Chocolate 24
Mouthwatering Cheesecake Milkshake 27
Savory Strawberries and Cream Milkshake 29
Galaxy Milkshake 31
Mocha Mint Milkshake 33
Cotton Candy Flavored Milkshake 35
Easy Peppermint Chocolate Chip Milkshake 37
Decadent Pumpkin Pie Milkshake 39
Earl Grey Honey Milkshakes 41
Savory Caramel Apple Milkshake 43
Classic Blueberry Milkshake 45
Candy Corn Milkshake 47
Creamy Nutella Milkshake 50
Delectable Chocolate Chip Cookie Dough Milkshake 52

Snickerdoodle Style Cookie Oatmeal Shake 55
Booze Packed Blueberry Pancake Milkshake........................... 57
Booze Packed Pumpkin Milkshake.. 60
Breakfast Style Blueberry Lavender and Honeycomb Milkshake
.... 62
Conclusion 64
About the Author 65
Author's Afterthoughts... 68

Introduction

Who isn't a huge fan of milkshakes? Whether you are a huge fan of vanilla, chocolate, malt chocolate, peanut butter, chocolate chip cookie dough, strawberry, pumpkin, caramel apples or even berry milkshakes, there is literally no end to the kind of milkshakes that you can make. Milkshakes are a great way to cool off during the summer holiday or just a treat to enjoy whenever you have a strong sweet tooth that you need to satisfy.

If you have been searching for a cookbook that can help you make some of the most delicious milkshake recipes ever, then you have certainly come to the right place. Inside of this book not only will use discover a variety of different combinations of shakes that you can make, but you will also discover a few popular milkshake recipes such as a chocolate chip cookie dough milkshake, pumpkin booze milkshake or even a mint chocolate chip cookie dough milkshake recipe.

So, let's not waste any more time. Let's get right into it!

Sweet Milkshake Recipes

Sweet Brownie Batter Milkshake

This is the perfect milkshake for those chocolate lovers out there. This milkshake recipes is packed full of creamy and savory chocolate flavor that will satisfy anybody's sweet tooth. Serve this with some chocolate whipped cream for the tastiest results.

Makes: 1 Serving

Total Prep Time: 5 Minutes

Ingredients:

- 1 ½ Cup of Ice Cream, Chocolate Flavored
- ½ Cup of Chocolate Milk, Cold
- 2 Tbsp. of Brownie Mix, Dried
- 2 Tbsp. of Brownie, Crumbled
- 1 Tbsp. of Chocolate Syrup
- Some Whipped Cream, Chocolate Flavored and For Topping
- Some Miniature Chocolate Chips, For Topping
- 1 Cherry, Maraschino, For Topping

Directions:

1. Add your all of your ingredients except for your chocolate style whipped cream, miniature chocolate chips and cherry into a blender.

2. Blend on the highest setting until smooth and creamy in consistency.

3. Pour your shake into a chilled milkshake glass. Top off with your chocolate chips, chocolate flavored whipped cream and your cherry right on top. Serve right away and enjoy.

Delicious Banana Foster Milkshake

If you are a huge fan of bananas, then this is the perfect milkshake recipe for you to make. It is sweet in taste and packed full of a savory banana taste, it makes for the perfect treat to enjoy during the summer holidays.

Makes: 1 Serving

Total Prep Time: 30 Minutes

Ingredients:

- 2 Bananas, Fresh and Peeled
- 1 Tbsp. of Lemon Juice, Fresh
- ¼ Cup of Sugar, Raw
- ¼ tsp. of Cinnamon, Ground Variety
- ½ tsp. of Banana Extract, Optional
- 1 tsp. of Rum Extract
- ¾ Cup of Milk, Whole
- 3 Cups of Ice Cream, Vanilla and Slightly Thawed
- 4 Strawberries, Rinsed, Hulled, Sliced Thinly and Garnish

Directions:

1. The first thing that you will want to do is preheat your oven. While your oven is heating up spray a medium sized baking dish with a generous amount of cooking spray. Set this dish aside.

2. Next slice your bananas in half and cut into small sized slices. Place your bananas into a small sized bowl along with your fresh lemon juice, raw sugar and ground cinnamon. Toss thoroughly to coat. Transfer this mixture into your baking dish.

3. Place into your oven to bake for the next 10 minutes or until soft to the touch. After this time remove your bananas from your oven and allow to cool completely.

4. Add your cooled banana mixture and all of your ingredients except for your strawberries into a blender.

5. Blend on the highest setting until smooth and creamy in consistency.

6. Pour your shake into a chilled milkshake glass. Top off with your strawberries. Serve right away and enjoy.

Classic Oreo Milkshake

If you are a huge fan of Oreos, then this is one milkshake recipe that you need to try making for yourself. For the tastiest results top your milkshake with one Oreo cookie for dipping or just to look appealing. Regardless, I know you are going to love it.

Makes: 1 Serving

Total Prep Time: 7 Minutes

Ingredients:

- 10 Oreo Cookies, Your Favorite Kind and Evenly Divided

- 3 Cups of Ice Cream, Vanilla Flavored
- ¾ Cup of Milk, Whole
- Some Chocolate Syrup, For Garnish
- Some Whipped Cream, For Garnish

Directions:

1. The first thing that you will want to do is chop 3 of your Oreo cookies finely to use as garnish. Set this aside for later use.

2. Add your remaining Oreo cookies and all of your ingredients except for your chocolate syrup and whipped cream into a blender.

3. Blend on the highest setting until smooth and creamy in consistency.

4. Drizzle your chocolate syrup down the sides of a chilled milkshake glass.

5. Pour your shake into a chilled milkshake glass. Top off with your whipped cream and serve right away.

Decadent Red Velvet Milkshake

There really isn't a time that you shouldn't enjoy this absolutely delicious milkshake recipe. It is a great tasting milkshake recipe to make whenever you are craving cake but don't want to go through the hassle of making it yourself.

Makes: 1 Serving

Total Prep Time: 5 Minutes

Ingredients:

- ½ Cup of Milk, Whole
- 1 ½ Cups of Ice Cream, Chocolate or Vanilla Flavored
- 2 Tbsp. of Cake Mix, Red Velvet Variety
- Some Whipped Cream, For Topping

Directions:

1. Add your all of your ingredients except for your whipped cream into a blender.

2. Blend on the highest setting until smooth and creamy in consistency.

3. Pour your shake into a chilled milkshake glass. Top off with your whipped cream and serve right away.

Chocolatey Mudslide Milkshake

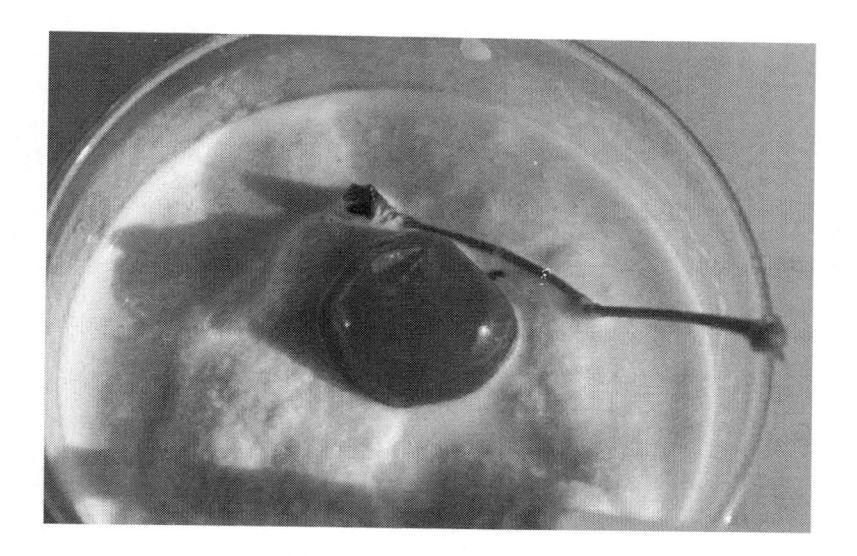

Looking for a milkshake dish that is more for adults? Then this is the perfect milkshake recipe for you to make. This is the perfect treat to make during your next party or gaming event to enjoy a great time in a tasty way.

Makes: 2 Servings

Total Prep Time: 10 Minutes

Ingredients:

- 2 Cups of Ice Cream, Vanilla Flavored
- 1 Tbsp. of Chocolate Syrup

- 2 Tbsp. of Chocolate, Powdered Variety
- 1 Cup of Ice
- 1 ½ Ounces of Liquor, Coffee Variety
- 1 ½ ounces of Irish Cream, Your Favorite Kind
- 1 ½ Ounces of Vodka, Your Favorite Kind

Directions:

1. First dip the rim of your chilled milkshake glasses into your chocolate sauce. Then dip in your powdered chocolate.

2. Lean your glass sideways and pour in your chocolate sauce while rotating the glass.

3. Next add your remaining ingredients into a blender.

4. Blend on the highest setting until smooth and creamy in consistency.

5. Pour your shake into your chilled milkshake glass. Top off with some whipped cream if you wish. Serve right away and enjoy.

Kit Kat Milkshake

This is a great milkshake recipe to make when you have an abundance of kit kats at your disposal around Halloween. It is a savory milkshake recipe to make that will surely satisfy all of your taste buds.

Makes: 2 Servings

Total Prep Time: 5 Minutes

Ingredients:

- 1 Kit Kat Bar, Broken Into Small Sized Pieces
- 2 Cups of Ice Cream, Vanilla Flavored
- ½ Cup of Milk, Whole
- 1 tsp. of Vanilla, Pure
- Some Chocolate Syrup, For Topping
- Some Whipped Cream, For Topping

Directions:

1. Add your all of your ingredients except for your whipped cream and chocolate syrup into a blender.

2. Blend on the highest setting until smooth and creamy in consistency.

3. Pour your shake into a chilled milkshake glass. Top off with your chocolate syrup and whipped cream. Serve right away and enjoy.

Sweet S'mores Milkshake

With the help of this milkshake you don't have to go out camping to enjoy delicious s'mores. Made with tasty chocolate, graham crackers and lightly toasted marshmallows. It is incredibly easy to make and absolutely delicious. I know you will love it.

Makes: 2 Servings

Total Prep Time: 30 Minutes

Ingredients for Your Chocolate Base:

- 7 ¾ Ounces of Chocolate Bars, Hershey and Evenly Divided

Ingredients for Your Whipped Cream:

- ½ Pint of Cream, Whipping Variety
- 1 tsp. of Vanilla, Pure
- 1 Tbsp. of Sugar, White in Color

Ingredients for Your Shake:

- 1 ½ Pints of Ice Cream, Vanilla Flavored
- 1 Cup of Milk, Whole
- ½ Cup of Graham Crackers, Crushed
- 1 Graham Cracker, Finely Crushed
- 1 ½ Ounces of Chocolate Bar, Hershey and Milk Variety
- 2 Tbsp. of Chocolate Syrup
- 2 Marshmallows, Large in Size

Directions:

1. First heat up your chocolate in a small sized bowl in your microwave until fully melted. Once melted place into your fridge to chill for the next 10 to 15 minutes or until thick in consistency. Set aside at least ½ a cup of this chocolate.

2. Spread a thin layer of your chocolate in a chilled milkshake glass. Dip the rim of your glass.

3. Next place your ice cream, whole milk, half a cup of your chocolate and graham crackers into a blender. Blend on the highest setting until smooth in consistency.

4. Spoon a scoop of ice cream into your chilled glass and pour your mixture over the top.

5. Place all of your ingredients for your whipped cream into a medium sized bowl. Beat with an electric mixer until fluffy in consistency. Pipe on top of your shake and sprinkle some graham crackers over the top. Top off with a drizzle of chocolate syrup.

6. Scorch your marshmallows under a broiler until charred and place in your milkshake. Enjoy right away.

Frozen Hot Chocolate

If you are a huge fan of hot chocolate like I am, then this is one milkshake recipe I know you are going to fall in love with. Even if you make this during the cold winter months, it may just help warm you up a bit.

Makes: 4 Servings

Total Prep Time: 10 Minutes

Ingredients:

- 5 Ounces of Chocolate, Dark in Color and Broken Into Small Sized Pieces
- ¼ Cup of Sugar, Granulated Variety
- 1 ½ Tbsp. of Cocoa Powdered Variety and Unsweetened
- 1 tsp. of Coffee Granules, Instant Variety
- 1 tsp. of Vanilla, Pure
- 2 Cups of Milk, Whole
- 4 Cups of Ice, Crushed
- Some Whipped Cream, For Topping
- Some Chocolate Sauce, For Topping
- Some Chocolate Curls, For Topping

Directions:

1. First add your dark chocolate, granulated sugar, powdered cocoa, instant coffee and at least one cup of milk into a small sized saucepot. Place over medium heat and stir thoroughly until your chocolate is fully melted and smooth in consistency. Remove from heat.

2. Pour your mixture into a blender along with your remaining milk, pure vanilla and crushed ice.

3. Blend on the highest setting until smooth and creamy in consistency.

4. Pour your shake into a chilled milkshake glass. Top off with your chocolate sauce, whipped cream and chocolate curls. Serve right away and enjoy.

Mouthwatering Cheesecake Milkshake

Whip up this tasty milkshake recipe whenever you are craving something to spoil yourself with. Made with only four ingredients, it really doesn't get any easier than this milkshake dish.

Makes: 3 Servings

Total Prep Time: 5 Minutes

Ingredients:

- 4 Ounces of Cream Cheese, Soft
- 1 Cup of Ice Cream, Vanilla Bean Variety
- ½ to ¾ Cup of Milk, Whole
- 1 Tbsp. of Graham Crackers, Crumbs and Some For Garnish
- Some Whipped Cream, For Topping
- Some Cherries, Maraschino Variety and For Topping

Directions:

1. Add your soft cream cheese, vanilla bean ice cream, your whole milk and graham cracker crumbs into a blender.

2. Blend on the highest setting until smooth and creamy in consistency.

3. Pour your shake into a chilled milkshake glass. Top off with your whipped cream, graham cracker crumbs and maraschino cherries. Serve right away and enjoy.

Savory Strawberries and Cream Milkshake

If you love the taste of milkshakes then this is one milkshake recipe that you need to try for yourself. This milkshake dish uses the ultimate combination of flavors to make a milkshake dish that I know you won't be able to resist.

Makes: 1 Serving

Total Prep Time: 5 Minutes

Ingredients:

- 1 Cup of Strawberries, Frozen and Sliced Thinly
- ½ Cup of Coffee Cream, French Vanilla Variety
- 1 Cup of Whipping Cream, Heavy Variety
- 1 Tbsp. of Sugar, White in Color

Directions:

1. Place your heavy whipping cream and sugar into a medium sized bowl. Use an electric mixer and beat on the highest setting until peaks begin to form. Transfer your whipped cream into a piping bag.

2. Then put your all of your ingredients into a blender.

3. Blend on the highest setting until smooth and creamy in consistency.

4. Pour your shake into a chilled milkshake glass. Top off with your freshly made whipped cream. Serve right away and enjoy.

Galaxy Milkshake

This is one milkshake recipe that even the pickiest of eaters will want to make over and over again. Vibrant with color and packed with the savory taste of vanilla, this is one delectable milkshake that you will love.

Makes: 1 Serving

Total Prep Time: 10 Minutes

Ingredients:

- 2 ½ Cups of Ice Cream, Vanilla Flavored
- ¾ to 1 Cup of Milk, Whole
- Some Food Coloring, Pink, Purple and Blue in Color
- Some Whipped Cream, For Topping
- Some Sprinkles, Pink, Purple and Blue in Color and For Topping

Directions:

1. First divide your ice cream and whole milk into three equal sized portions.

2. Blend each portion in your blender separately along with three individual portions of your food coloring.

3. After each portion has been blender pour each into a chilled glass.

4. Top off with some whipped cream and your multicolored sprinkles. Serve right away and enjoy.

Mocha Mint Milkshake

If you are looking for something more on the filling side when it comes to shakes, then this is one recipe you can't go wrong with. It is perfect to make during the hot summer months and will leave you feeling refreshed for hours.

Makes: 2 to 4 Servings

Total Prep Time: 5 Minutes

Ingredients:

- 4 Cups of Ice Cream, Mint Chocolate Chip Variety
- ½ Cup of Syrup, Chocolate Variety
- ½ Cup of Coffee, Cold and Strong

- ½ Cup of Milk, Whole

- ¼ Cup of Chocolate Syrup, For Topping

- ¼ Cup of Mints, Andes Variety

- Some Whipped Cream, For Garnish

Directions:

1. First add your chocolate chip style ice cream, cold coffee, chocolate syrup and whole milk into a blender.

2. Blend on the highest setting until smooth and creamy in consistency.

3. Then take your chilled milkshake glasses and pour in your chocolate syrup along the sides while rotating the glass in the process.

4. Pour your shake into a chilled milkshake glass. Top off with your Andes style mints and whipped cream. Serve right away and enjoy.

Cotton Candy Flavored Milkshake

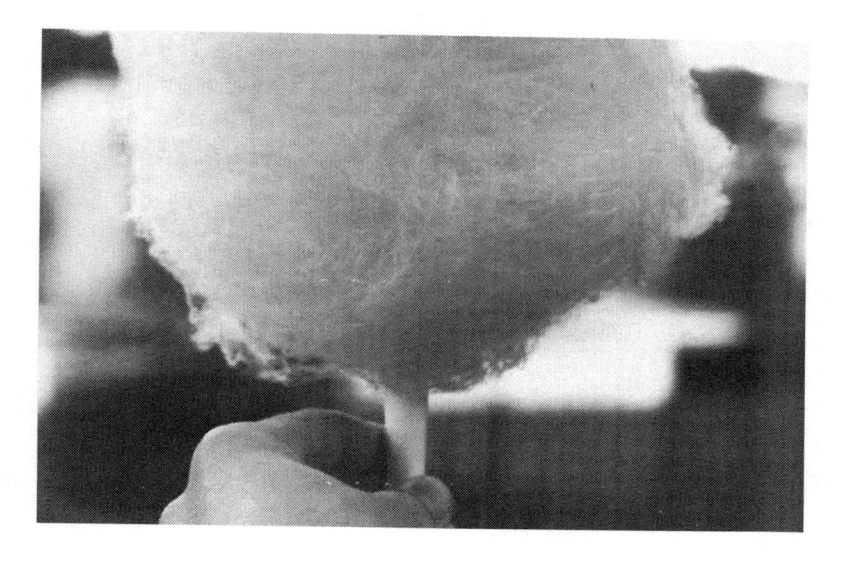

There is nothing else on the planet that can quite bring out your inner child than cotton candy itself. Well, with the use of this recipe you can enjoy the wonderful taste of cotton candy without having to visit your local fair.

Makes: 1 Serving

Total Prep Time: 5 Minutes

Ingredients:

- 2 Cups of Ice Cream, Cotton Candy Flavored
- ½ Cup of Cotton Candy, Fresh
- ¼ Cup of Milk, Whole
- Some Extra Cotton Candy, For Garnish

Directions:

1. Add your all of your ingredients except for your extra cotton candy into a blender.

2. Blend on the highest setting until smooth and creamy in consistency.

3. Pour your shake into a chilled milkshake glass. Top off with a garnish of your extra cotton candy. Serve right away and enjoy.

Easy Peppermint Chocolate Chip Milkshake

If you are looking for a simple milkshake recipe that will help get you into the holiday spirit, then this is the perfect milkshake dish for you to make. For the tastiest results, don't hesitate to drop a candy cane right into the glass!

Makes: 2 Servings

Total Prep Time: 5 Minutes

Ingredients:

- 2 Cups of Ice Cream, Vanilla Flavored
- ½ Cup of Milk, Whole
- 1 to 2 tsp. of Peppermint Extract, Pure
- 4 Candy Canes, Crushed
- ¼ Cup of Chocolate Chips, Semi Sweet Variety
- Some Whipped Cream, For Topping
- Some Candy Canes, Crushed and For Topping

Directions:

1. Add your all of your ingredients except for your whipped cream and crushed candy canes into a blender.

2. Blend on the highest setting until smooth and creamy in consistency.

3. Pour your shake into a chilled milkshake glass. Top off with your whipped cream and crushed candy canes as a garnish. Serve right away and enjoy.

Decadent Pumpkin Pie Milkshake

This is the perfect milkshake to make when pumpkins begin to come into season and you are starting to pumpkinfy everything! It is a great tasting milkshake recipe to make to celebrate the changing of the season.

Makes: 2 Servings

Total Prep Time: 5 Minutes

Ingredients:

- 2 Cups of Ice Cream, Vanilla Flavored
- 1 Cup of Milk, Whole
- ½ Cup of Pumpkin, Pureed
- 1 Tbsp. of Pumpkin Pie Spice
- ¼ Cup of Graham Cracker Crumbs
- Some Whipped Cream, For Topping
- Some Graham Cracker Crumbs, For Topping

Directions:

1. Add your all of your ingredients except for your whipped cream and graham cracker crumbs into a blender.

2. Blend on the highest setting until smooth and creamy in consistency.

3. Pour your shake into a chilled milkshake glass. Top off with your whipped cream and graham cracker crumbs as a garnish. Serve right away and enjoy.

Earl Grey Honey Milkshakes

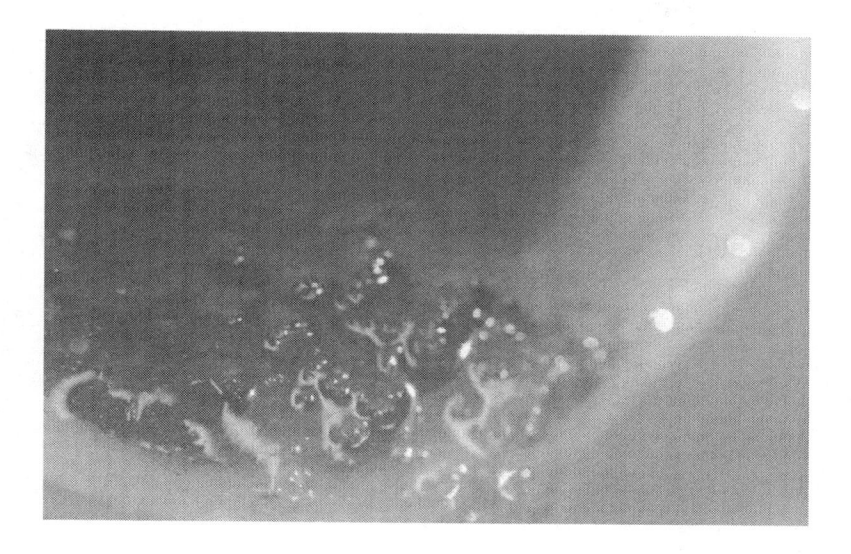

Here is a delicious milkshake recipe to make whenever you are looking for something on the English side. Thick and creamy in consistency, this milkshake incorporates the perfect combination of milk, honey and English tea, making a savory milkshake to enjoy whenever you wish.

Makes: 3 to 4 Servings

Total Prep Time: 35 Minutes

Ingredients:

- 4 Tbsp. of Tea, Earl Grey Variety and Loose Leaf Variety

- 1 ½ Cups of Water, Boiling
- 1 Cup of Ice Cream, Vanilla Flavored
- ¾ Cup of Half and Half
- 2 Tbsp. of Honey, Raw
- 12 Ice Cubes, Whole

Directions:

1. The first thing that you will want to do is steep your tea in your boiling water for at least 4 minutes. After this time strain your tea and set aside to cool for the next 20 minutes.

2. Net add your vanilla ice cream and half and half into a blender.

3. Blend on the highest setting until smooth and creamy in consistency.

4. Add in your Earl Grey Tea and honey. Blend again until evenly incorporated. Add in your ice and blend again until smooth in consistency.

5. Pour your shake into a chilled milkshake glass. Serve right away and enjoy.

Savory Caramel Apple Milkshake

This is the perfect milkshake recipe to make when apples are coming into season and you can pick them fresh yourself. It is incredibly easy to make and tastes absolutely delicious, this is the perfect milkshake recipe to make for those picky children in your household.

Makes: 1 Serving

Total Prep Time: 5 Minutes

Ingredients:

- 2 Cups of Ice Cream, Vanilla Flavored
- 1 ½ Cups of Cider, Apple Variety
- 1 Apple, Granny Smith Variety, Peeled, Cored and Finely Chopped
- ¼ Cup of Caramel Sauce
- Some Whipped Cream, For Topping

Directions:

1. Add your vanilla ice cream, apple cider and chopped granny style apple into a blender.

2. Blend on the highest setting until smooth and creamy in consistency.

3. Pour your shake into a chilled milkshake glass. Top off with your caramel sauce and your whipped cream. Serve right away and enjoy.

Classic Blueberry Milkshake

There is no other classic milkshake quite like this classic blueberry milkshake. Packed full of a delicious blueberry taste that I know you won't be able to get enough of. Not only is it incredibly delicious, but it is highly beneficial for you as well.

Makes: 1 Serving

Total Prep Time: 5 Minutes

Ingredients:

- 2 Cups of Ice Cream, Vanilla Flavored and Your Favorite Kind
- 2 Cups of Blueberries, Fresh or Frozen
- 2 Cups of Milk, Whole
- 1 Tbsp. of Honey, Raw

Directions:

1. Add your vanilla flavored ice cream, fresh or frozen blueberries, whole milk and raw honey into a blender.

2. Blend on the highest setting until smooth and creamy in consistency.

3. Pour your shake into a chilled milkshake glass. Top off with some whipped cream and a few blueberries on top if you wish. Serve right away and enjoy.

Candy Corn Milkshake

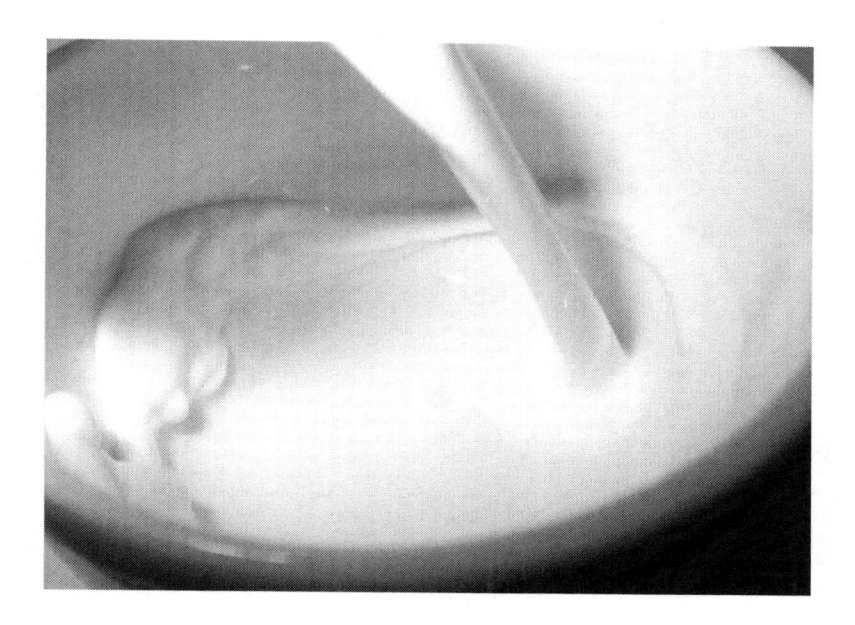

If you are craving something on the sweeter side during the Halloween season, then this is the perfect milkshake for you to make. The fanta drink that you will use in this recipe helps to give this milkshake a bit of a kick that you won't be able to resist for long.

Makes: 2 Servings

Total Prep Time: 10 Minutes

Ingredients:

- ¼ Cup of Fanta, Pineapple Flavored
- ¼ Cup of Fanta, Orange Flavored
- ½ Cup of Milk, Whole
- 1 Cup of Sherbet, Orange Variety
- 1 Cup of Sherbet, Yellow Variety
- 1 Scoop of Ice Cream, Vanilla Flavored
- 1 to 2 Drops of Food Coloring, Red in Color
- 1 to 2 Drops of Food Coloring, Yellow in Color
- Some Whipped Cream, For Topping
- Some Sprinkle, Yellow and Orange in Color and For Topping

Directions:

1. First add your yellow sherbet, pineapple flavored Fanta and drops of yellow food coloring into a blender. Blend on the highest setting until smooth in consistency. Pour this portion into the bottom of a chilled milkshake glass.

2. Then add in your orange flavored Fanta, orange sherbet and drop of yellow food coloring into a blender. Blend on the highest setting until smooth in consistency. Pour this over your yellow layer of shake in your milkshake glass.

3. Next add your vanilla ice cream and milk into your blender. Blend on the highest setting until smooth in consistency. Pour on top of your orange layer in your milkshake glass.

4. Top your milkshake off with your whipped cream and multicolored sprinkles. Serve right away and enjoy.

Creamy Nutella Milkshake

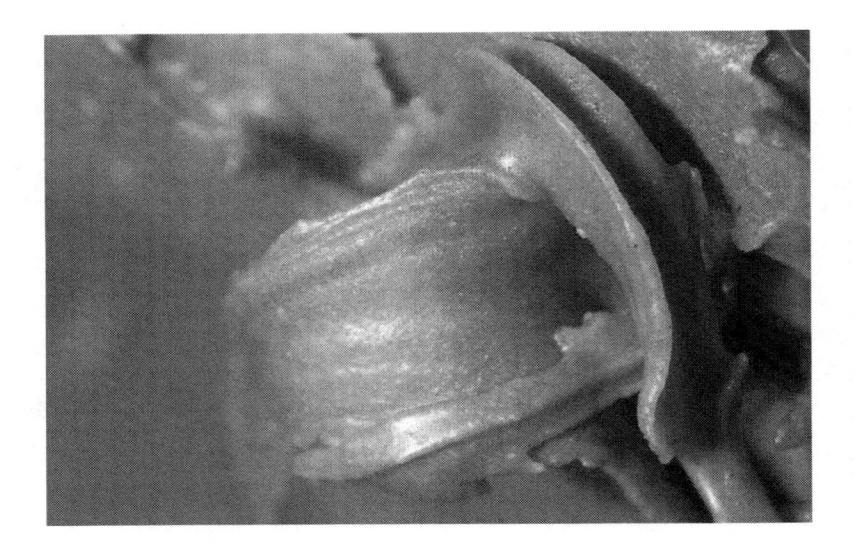

If you are a huge fan of Nutella, then this is one milkshake dish that you will want to try making for yourself. This delicious milkshake is made with fresh Nutella, chocolate flavored milk and creamy ice cream to make a milkshake that you are going to want to make over and over again.

Makes: 2 Servings

Total Prep Time: 5 Minutes

Ingredients:

- 2 ½ Cups of Ice Cream, Chocolate Flavored and Evenly Divided
- 1/3 Cup of Nutella
- ¼ Cup of Milk, Chocolate Variety
- 2 Ounces of Vodka, Your Favorite Kind
- 2 Ounces of Crème de Cacao
- Some Whipped Cream, For Topping
- Some Caramel Sauce, For Topping

Directions:

1. Add in all of your ingredients except for your whipped cream and caramel sauce into a blender.

2. Blend on the highest setting until smooth and creamy in consistency.

3. Pour your shake into a chilled milkshake glass. Top off with your whipped cream and drizzle your caramel sauce over the top. Serve right away and enjoy.

Delectable Chocolate Chip Cookie Dough Milkshake

Here is yet another absolutely delicious chocolate chip cookie dough milkshake I know you are going to want to make over and over again. There is nothing quite like this milkshake out there and once you get a taste of it yourself, you are going to want to make it as frequently as possible.

Makes: 2 Servings

Total Prep Time: 10 Minutes

Ingredients:

- 1 ¼ cup of Milk, Whole
- 4 Cups of Ice Cream, Vanilla Flavored
- 1 Cup of Cookie Dough, Premade Variety
- ½ Cup of Chocolate Chips
- Some Whipped Cream, For Topping
- ½ Cup of Cookie Dough, Premade Variety and For Garnish
- 1/3 Cup of Chocolate Chips, Milk Variety and For Garnish
- 1 Chocolate Chip Cookie, For Garnish

Directions:

1. The first thing that you will want to do is add your cookie dough to the rim of your milkshake glasses. Then roll in your milk chocolate chips. Place into your freezer to freeze until you are ready to use it.

2. Then add your whole milk, vanilla ice cream, premade cookie dough and remaining chocolate chips into a blender.

3. Blend on the highest setting until smooth and creamy in consistency.

4. Pour your shake into a chilled milkshake glass. Top off with your whipped cream and your cookie right on top. Serve right away and enjoy.

Snickerdoodle Style Cookie Oatmeal Shake

If you are a huge fan of snickerdoodles, then this is the perfect milkshake recipe for you to make. Sweet to take and made in just a matter of minutes, you will be able to satisfy your strongest sweet tooth before you know it.

Makes: 1 Serving

Total Prep Time: 5 Minutes

Ingredients:

- 2/3 Cup of Milk, Almond Variety
- 1/3 Cup of Oats
- 1 Banana, Large in Size and Frozen
- 1 Tbsp. of Butter, Almond Variety
- ½ Tbsp. of Syrup, Maple Variety
- ½ tsp. of Cinnamon, Ground Variety
- ¼ tsp. of Vanilla, Pure
- Pinch of Baker's Style Baking Soda
- Dash of Salt, For Taste
- One Snickerdoodle Cookie, For Garnish

Directions:

1. Add all of your ingredients except for your snickerdoodle cookie into a blender.

2. Blend on the highest setting until smooth and creamy in consistency.

3. Pour your shake into a chilled milkshake glass. Top off with some whipped cream and your snickerdoodle cookie. Serve right away and enjoy.

Booze Packed Blueberry Pancake Milkshake

This milkshake taste identical to a blueberry pancake. With that in mind it is the perfect milkshake to make in the morning or whenever you have a strong sweet tooth that needs to be satisfied.

Makes: 2 Servings

Total Prep Time: 9 Minutes

Ingredients for Your Blueberry Syrup:

- 1/3 Cup of Blueberries, Fresh
- 1 ½ Tbsp. of Sugar, White in Color

Ingredients for Your Milkshake:

- 1 Pint of Ice Cream, Vanilla Flavored
- 1/3 Cup + 2 Tbsp. of Vodka, Blueberry Flavored
- ½ Cup of Milk, Whole
- 2 tsp. of Butter, Extract and Pure
- 3 Tbsp. of Maple Syrup, Your Favorite Kind

Directions:

1. The first thing that you will want to do is make your blueberry syrup. To do this place your blueberries with your sugar into a small sized skillet placed over medium heat. Cook until the juice begin to come out of your blueberries.

2. Remove from heat and mash your blueberries thoroughly. Continue to cook until your juice is thick in consistency.

3. Strain your sauce through a fine mesh strainer and set aside to cool for later use.

4. Add in all of your ingredients for your milkshake into a blender.

5. Blend on the highest setting until smooth and creamy in consistency.

6. Pour your fresh blueberry sauce along the sides of a chilled milkshake glass and pour your shake into your glass as well. Top off with some whipped cream if you wish. Serve right away and enjoy.

Booze Packed Pumpkin Milkshake

Here is yet another pumpkin recipe I know the average adult is going to fall in love with. Packed full of that pumpkin taste mixed with a bit of alcohol, this is one recipe you are going to want to make whenever you are craving something alcoholic.

Makes: 2 Servings

Total Prep Time: 10 Minutes

Ingredients:

- ¼ Cup of Caramel Sauce, Warm

- ½ Cup of Graham Cracker Crumbs, Lightly Toasted
- 1 Pint of Ice Cream, Vanilla Flavored
- 6 Tbsp. of Pumpkin, Pureed
- ½ tsp. of Pumpkin Pie Spice
- 1 tsp. of Cinnamon, Ground
- 3 Tbsp. of Milk, Whole
- ¼ Cup of Bourbon

Directions:

1. First place your graham cracker crumbs onto a small sized flat plate. Wet the rim of your glass with some water and dip in your graham cracker crumbs.

2. Drizzle your caramel sauce along the sides of the inside of two chilled milkshake glasses.

3. Add in your vanilla flavored ice cream, pureed pumpkin, bourbon, ground cinnamon, pumpkin pie spice and whole milk into a blender.

4. Blend on the highest setting until smooth and creamy in consistency.

5. Pour your shake into your chilled milkshake glasses. Top off with some whipped cream if you wish. Serve right away and enjoy.

Breakfast Style Blueberry Lavender and Honeycomb Milkshake

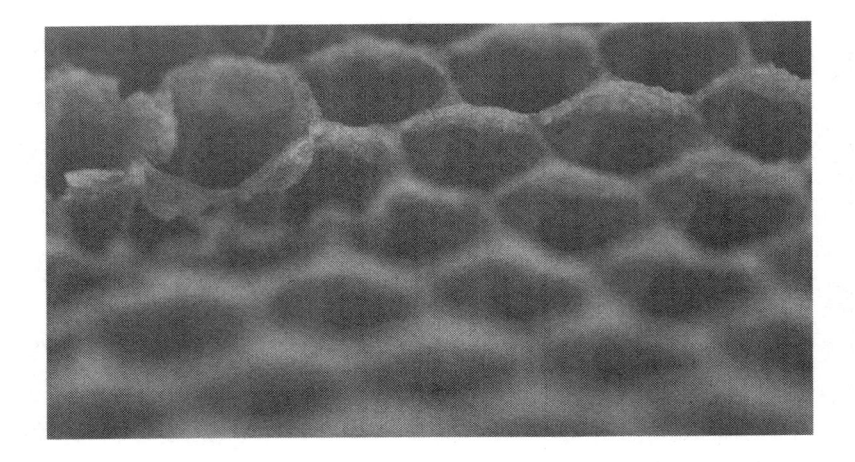

If you are looking for a quick and satisfying breakfast dish to make to take with you on the way out the door in the morning, then this is the perfect milkshake recipe for you to make. Ready in just a matter of minutes, this is ideal for those who need breakfast in a hurry.

Makes: 2 Servings

Total Prep Time: 35 Minutes

Ingredients:

- 2 Cups of Yogurt, Greek Variety
- 1 Cup 0of Blueberries, Fresh or Frozen
- 1 Cup of Milk, Coconut Variety
- 1 Tbsp. of lemon Juice, Fresh
- 1 tsp. of Lavender, Buds Only
- ½ tsp. of Vanilla, Pure
- 1 Pack of Honeycomb

Directions:

1. The first thing that you will want to do is place your yogurt into a medium sized bowl and set into your freezer to freeze for the next 30 minutes.

2. Add in all of your ingredients including your Greek style yogurt into a blender.

3. Blend on the highest setting until smooth and creamy in consistency.

4. Pour your shake into a chilled milkshake glass. Top off with some whipped cream if you prefer. Serve right away and enjoy.

Conclusion

Well, there you have it!

Hopefully by the end of this book not only have you learned how to make some of the most delicious milkshake recipe you can craft in your imagination, but you have also learned how to do so using your favorite kind of ingredients. I also hope that the over 25 different milkshake recipes that you have access to will help you to do just that.

So, what is next for you?

The next step for you to take is to begin making all of these delicious milkshake recipes for yourself. Remember, don't hesitate to use your favorite kind of ingredients or topping to make milkshake recipes that you won't be able to resist.

Good luck!

About the Author

Hello my name is Ted Alling,

For as long as I can remember, I have always loved cooking and spending time in the kitchen. I honestly thought that my mother had dedicated her life to cooking, but later on in life, I came to understand that she was just a great stay at home mom of 4. Although I was a boy, I was always the only one interested in helping my mom make pancakes, fried eggs, and bratwurst. She proceeded to teach me how to make pasta, to cook chicken, stuff cabbages, and even how to make a pretty good risotto.

Life in Germany was wonderful as a kid, but my parents decided to move to the United States, or more specifically to the state of Illinois, in 1990. When I moved out to go to college in Georgia, not only was I able to make some delicious dishes, but I was a very popular roommate to have—I was one of the very rare ones who could prepare something other than mac & cheese from the box. The other students from the dorm really dug my special fried rice. Until this day, I won't give out the secret ingredient that makes it unique…

I graduated from college with honors and an accounting degree in 1995, and soon after started working in a firm in downtown Atlanta. All I could think about all day was what I would make for my girlfriend for dinner. She obviously did not mind that I had taken over the kitchen early on in our relationship. She is a nurse, and often has to work long hours and comes home exhausted and hungry.

However, food had become much more than a hobby or necessity for me…it was actually closer to an obsession, but I prefer to use the term passion. I was spending most of my weekends visiting fresh local markets and discovering new produce and herbs. After working as an accountant for 5 years, I realized that life was far too short to continue missing out on my true calling: cooking.

I applied as a part time cook at a local diner about 10 minutes from home, and the rest, as they say, is history. Three years later I was opening my own restaurant with my wife as my main partner. All my ex-fellow accountants now come in to eat at lunch time. We have been serving our clientele my famous fried rice, and many more dishes that I will be glad to share with you over the future weeks.

What makes me a good chef? My passion for food, and the fresher the ingredients, the better. I love to experiment with flavors and I dare you to do the same. Sure, we all have our favorites, but don't settle in your ways. Be creative. Play with the colors, the herbs, the spices, the types of meat, fruits, and vegetables. Grow your own garden and talk to your butcher about trying different cuts of meat that he has to offer on a weekly basis.

Now, I have to go back to the kitchen, but next time you feel like preparing a mouthwatering dish, please stop by, and I will make sure to share "most" of my secrets.

Author's Afterthoughts

Thanks ever so much to each of my cherished readers for investing the time to read this book!

I know you could have picked from many other books but you chose this one. So a big thanks for downloading this book and reading all the way to the end.

If you enjoyed this book or received value from it, I'd like to ask you for a favor. Please take a few minutes to post an honest and heartfelt review on Amazon.com. Your support does make a difference and helps to benefit other people.

Thanks!

Ted Alling

Made in the USA
Middletown, DE
03 September 2017